Is

There

Not A

Is There Not A Cause?

Nathaniel Terrell

atmosphere press

Published by Atmosphere Press

Cover design by Nick Courtright

atmospherepress.com

Dedicated to Kayden (Butter bean). Don't let anything or anyone stop you from achieving whatever it is that you choose to pursue in life. I love you nephew.

Table of Contents

Foreword

The super-storm has come and gone
the devastation was massive
and almost fatal
However,
the waters have receded and the destructive winds are gone
The incredible damage has been done
now, I stare at the broken fragments of my life
and in this immense after-math
like any after-math
a man can either move on
or he can stand firm and rebuild
I chose to rebuild
So much was taken away
Fortunately I was left
with all that I need
God is great!
This world is nuts!
Now, the time is!

Long Shot

I can't smoke it away, I can't drink it away
it reaches me even in my sleep
the fury in my chest scorches like lava
I find it difficult to breathe
my heart is beating like a war drum
I feel light-headed but I won't panic
I close my eyes and slowly slip far away
from the noise and anger
To a place where I can think, strategize and focus
clinging to hope, in this moment, it is here
that I take a long shot through the darkness
A surplus of emotions create a perfect storm
a deadly storm, the quiet storm
I feel everything and at the same time I feel nothing
Heaven help us all
Racism, intolerance and bigotry are alive and well
ignorance and hate have platforms
that speak to a large audience
Domestic terrorist shooters target
mass innocent unassuming bodies
We are tormented by radical extremists, COVID19,
 chemical warfare, sexual misconduct, exploitation and rape
horrifying natural disasters
and undetected bombs unleash atrocious devastation
to crowded metro centers around the world
Heaven help us all
Self-hate multiplies
and divides my people further
The call for immigration reform is loud and echoing
while lies are well told and souls are being sold
A true House of God
can't serve as a cover-up for a den for thieves
I won't dance and celebrate
while my brothers are in need
Many perform in the pulpit
but how many will preach in the streets?
I fight against myself daily

I feel lost but I know my breakthrough is within my reach
Heaven help us all
Family over everything
I struggle to be a better man
no longer the man I was
and not yet the man I will be
Throughout this journey I balance
passion, pain, purpose
premonitions and prayer
Happiness starts within
every new day is a blessing
the process will never be sweet
However, here I stand
I speak life
I will rise above failure
I will succeed beyond adversity
Father forgive us
Heaven help us all

Cross Roads

Don't know if I will see heaven
still I humbly grace your throne

I battle vices, doubt, this path and myself
I am living wrong
I hold onto my birthright my word and balls
holding all three in high esteem

Darkness rises and overshadows
yet and still I believe
I cover miles
while I am tired
Tribulations trap the weak
and test the strong
Through many failures
I've gained a measure of wisdom
Until I expire I will keep holding on

Hands Of War

Regardless of the outcome
be it triumph or heartbreak

I will stand with a straight back
chest out and my head held high

This journey has been long and eventful
the highs were like soaring above an eagle
and the lows deep as the pits of hell

Tonight I sit beside a large brook
I gaze into the water
and I appreciate the splendor of the night sky

I see the reflection of a full moon
brightened by a plethora of stars
I disrupt the perfect picture
as I put my dirty, sweaty hands
in the cool water

The wonderful sounds
of the night creatures overtake my ears
while I bask in their sweet serenade

Tonight is peaceful
I enjoy every second of serenity
in this moment of bliss I meditate
and I enjoy the elements as they welcome me

I give thanks and I offer up praise
for blessings, grace, and protection
after I disrobe, I bathe
washing blood from my face, body, and sword

I step out the water, clean and refreshed
and before I take rest

I cherish the solace in this late-night hour
Dawn will usher in a new day
and I will continue on this gruesome road
Deep in this war that I will not run or hide from
and I am content regardless of the out-come
be it triumph or my demise

Twelve years a writer

If seeking approval/validation is why you do what you do
then by all means do that

We all want likes, subscribers, shares, and followers
there's nothing wrong with that

But please keep in mind that whatever gift, calling, talent
or purpose you operate in will still be there
whether the masses feel you or not

Be confident in yourself and your abilities
good success will not come easy or without sacrifice and failures

And as with any advice
words spoken over your life, criticism or negative feedback
chew the meat and spit out the bones

Haters and detractors will always be with us
and often times those that hate you the most
can't do what you do or operate on your level

If ever you feel like throwing in the towel
or that you're ineffective, just remember

If you are able to reach just one person
your purpose has been validated

And if you can help one,
then odds are you will help others
so keep grinding, keep creating, have fun with it

Put the hard work in and your time will come
Be encouraged! Stay safe! Do well!

Just Like That

A double-minded man
is unstable in all his ways

We as brothers face opposition
if we decide to grow locks
but if we put on a dress
receive opportunities, adulation, and fame

I refuse to make promises
I have no intent to keep

Hold my actions accountable
to the words that I speak

Being a strong, proud man
the principalities that rule
target me as a threat

And as a man
I war with rejection
injustice, gate keepers and regret

No man is an island
yet and still
I walk alone

I am not lost
just went the wrong way
now, I am making my way back home

Just as the sun
cuts the dark in the morning
every time life knocks me down, I will rise

Through over standing
I will battle the legacy of Willie Lynch
and honor my ancestors
by keeping my eyes on the prize

Time is priceless
the time to stand is now
time will always tell

Brothers and Sisters
we are mighty children
of the Universal God

Love one another
but first love yourself

Smoke & Praise

Hear my declaration of praise
through this smoke and haze

Pain my nemesis
my greatest motivator
I study the man in mirror and lock eyes with my greatest foe

Driven with unbridled passion
an inferno burns within

My faith is shaken but not broken
I defy inner voices of doubt

I fear not reaching my full potential
I pray that favor stays on my side

Failure mocks me
success stalks me

But as I make my way through
all the smoke and haze
I offer the Most High a declaration of praise

Only In Dreams

Love asked for one reason
my answer was two

You've accepted my idiosyncrasies
and I'm fine with the flaws in you

Loyalty, understanding
and patience
keeps us growing together and strong

Our harmony
amplifies the melody
of a healing heart's song

It is my duty to make you smile,
love you right and keep you happy
from year to year

You make my world
heaven on earth
I am so grateful that you are here

You are beyond beautiful
we share a healthy sense of a humor
and the love you give is more than enough

But reality is a cruel reminder
because you vanish
every morning when I wake up

Have Mercy

I keep falling down
as I try to find my way
I am thankful for strength, good health
and seeing a brand new day

Yes Lord

I read scriptures
and pray to get delivered
I paint pictures through lyrics
as the beat moves quicker

Yes Lord, and I am paying penance
Lord forgive me for my sins
for my failures, my ambitions
and for when I sin again

Yes Lord

I keep chasing love
as my heart defies my brain
I play the devil's advocate
yet I pray in Jesus name

Help me Lord
Yes Lord

Greatness lies within me
I fight demons that lie beneath
my vices are substitutes
for the happiness I seek

Yes Lord

Am I the author of chaos?
When is enough, enough?
Will I ever move with caution?

Will I ever give a fuck?

Take me to the king
to the place where I first found him
Nightmares haunt my sleep
for tomorrow is not promised?

Yes Lord
Yes Lord

,

Shattered Dreams

Cursed is he who hangs from the tree
Inadequacy, failure, and shame for all to see
Had so much potential but never reached his peak
Was so good with hands, covered many miles on his feet
A tragic story of what could have been and what will never be
The legion of voices are now silent, I pray he rests in peace
He would fall and get back up a tormentors repeat
He fought like a warrior until his defeat
Made in God's image but inner demons dwelt deep
Cursed is he who hangs from the tree

Message

Pause
breathe
pray

Study to be quiet
there's power in all that we say

Fight, fight, fight
everything that stands in your way

Appreciate life
a body will be buried today

If you can emerge from the dirt
there's no reason you can't fly

Do not live in fear
look every man in his eyes

Cherish your laughs
sometimes you'll have to cry

Guard your steps
if the Devil exists
how can it be a lie?

I Never Knew

I never knew I'd become a lone wolf only to miss my team

I never knew rejections would motivate me to capture my dreams

I never knew I was a champion until I lost the fight

I never knew how wrong I was until I saw what was right

I never knew I'd remember until I forgot

I never knew what little I had would manifest into a lot

I never knew the things I once cherished, I would now despise

I never knew desire until I looked in your eyes

I never knew how significant home was until I got lost

I never knew I'd brand a career until I got sick of my job

I never knew consecration until the curse was reversed

I never knew I'd do my best when I was at my worst

I never knew I'd miss sunshine until I almost drowned in the rain

I never knew that one day I would get past the pain

I never knew that fire was meant to go through

I never knew that I'd ever find someone like you

I never knew that I would find bliss

and learn so much from all

that I never knew

Memory Lane

Pain or pleasure
was it addiction, love or lust?
We had a mighty bond
until we shattered trust
As I look deep in your eyes
you can see I'm not the same
We fell out long ago
but I'm really glad you came
The vibe was nice
as we danced down memory lane
Now that the suns come up
we must go our separate ways

End Game

The sheep follow fads
man-made icons and the latest sensations
too often death is the end game
for instant gratification

Greedy rats fill their bellies
while being stalked by hungry owls
Judgment often shows no mercy
its strike is cold and foul

Warnings are all around us
we often ignore the signs

We can get back a lot of things that were lost
but we can never replace time

The undercurrent of hate is ignorance
and in many jealousy and envy run deep
there will always be degrees of power
so no there will never be peace

As morality crumbles the future is shortened
and fools believe they are wise
the perverse impose, standards are lowered
and poison infiltrates our minds

History repeats itself, the ignorant perish
and tragedy invokes change
Unity is unstoppable, awareness preserves
and life is not a game

Right Now

I'm alright
Oh yes I am
life beat me down
But look here I stand
I'll make the most
of this second chance

It is alright
Yes I'm alright

I said I'm alright
Baby yes I am
I've come so far
and I won't go back
Lets help heal the world
as we march hand in hand

Let's make it alright
Yeah I'm alright

Just Thought I'd Share That With You

Deacon Jones: Nathaniel, why do I smell gas? And what are you doing with that torch?

Me: I need the gas and torch to put something to rest.

Deacon Jones: Son, you just can't get right. After all these years, you're still playing with fire.

Me: Pop this time I'm right. And I'm not playing with fire, I'm using it.

Deacon Jones: And what did I tell you about smoking those cigarettes?

Me: Well Pop, you told me a lot but I'm trying to quit smoking and this ain't a cigarette, this is a tip.

Deacon Jones: Oh, well look at you. You know something that I don't.

Me: I know the difference between a cigar and a cigarette.

Deacon Jones: Boy I'm not going to stand here and compare apples and oranges with you.

Me: I didn't mean it like that Pop.

Deacon Jones: Look at me when I'm talking to you. Why do you keep staring at that bridge behind you?

Me; See Pops that's what I'm trying to tell you.

Deacon Jones: Lord have mercy, you're about to burn that bridge, aren't you?

Me: Pops when you're right, you're right.

Deacon Jones: I don't know where your mother and I went wrong with you. And I'll tell you another thing...

Me: Pop, just hear me out.

Deacon Jones: Thank you, Jesus! This don't make no sense, you know what, go ahead Son tell me what you want me to hear.

Me: Daddy, the bridge is behind me, right?

Deacon Jones: Yeah so what?

Me: Well the way I see it, I'm moving forward.

Deacon Jones: Well you were but now you're back to playing with fire.

Me: Pops, I wasn't finished.

Deacon Jones: Phew...go ahead, Nathaniel.

Me: Now like I was saying before I was so rudely interrupted.

Deacon Jones: Watch it boy, you think I'm too old to go upside your head?

Me: No sir, may I continue?

Deacon Jones: That's better, I'm listening.

Me: Pop, that bridge leads back to where I came from and if I'm moving forward I am not going back. That bridge leads to misery, heartache, and pain. So I'm about to torch it, to ensure that I never ever go that way again.

Deacon Jones: Well my goodness, you aren't quite as stupid as you look and a lot of times act.

Me:(sarcastically) Well I love you too Pop.

Deacon Jones: Well what are you looking at me for? If that's how you feel burn it down!

Me: Okay. (I throw the torch on the bridge, flames engulf it)

Me: Isn't that fire beautiful Dad?

Deacon Jones: Son, your mother is beautiful. All that is, is fire.

Me: Come on, Pop!

Deacon Jones: Come on Pop nothing. Now I know you moving forward and everything but boy it's cold out here let me give you a ride.

Me: Alright Pop, Why are you staring at me like that?

Deacon Jones: Now I know you know better than to think you are getting in this truck with that cigar, tip or whatever it is. Put it out!

Me: Yes Dad.

Deacon Jones: Come on Son, you are something else!

Me: I know I am, so are you Pop.

Deacon Jones: (laughing) Now put your seat-belt on and don't touch my radio or my heater.

Me: I won't Pop.

Deacon Jones: You bet not.

Deacon Jones: Yeah Son, the Good Lord is blessing.

Me: He sure is Pop

Let Go

Hey love,
dry your eyes and fix that pretty face
I understand why you're still holding on

Some things are difficult to let go
and the thought of falling can strike fear
but the beauty of it all is

Once you let go
you give yourself an opportunity
to grow and reach heights you haven't fathomed

But I am certain you already know this
so, why beloved
do you continue to hold on
to the very thing that holds you back?

Outsider

And it hit deep in my soul
like a mid-nineties R&B love song
and being raised old school
I am extremely out of my element

As I convey the carnage all around me
I am pained to realize that
the beautiful plan I concocted
has gone horribly awry

I wish I had the tears to weep without restraint
because it is apparent that life as I know it
 will never be the same again

And in these fleeting last moments
that I live as the man I have always been
before I am forced to adapt to the harsh reality
that I alone created with my cursed reckless ambition

And at the very least become a scavenger
lest I succumb to this dreaded situation and perish
I humble myself and strip naked out of my ego and pride

I became a victim to the lusts of my eyes and flesh
and to be honest my vanity
 has entrapped me

I pray to God for the fortitude
endurance and wit
to turn this awful predicament
into a rewarding process

Where I rise above the shadow of death
to levitate over the flames
of disaster, failure, and defeat
And ascend through a stratosphere
few have breached

Ain't Shit

What do you do
when deadly results occur
from good intentions?

Respect is great
once earned
but a sad affair when lost

Deceit can easily
shatter bonds
thought to be unbreakable

I seek forgiveness
and wash my hands everyday
only Jesus can wash my sins away

I won't jump out a window
but I'll climb over this gate

I'll love you forever
but I will never
love you enough to stay

Dry Bones
(Shout out to KRS for revealing G.U.N.)

I am the detached survivor
of what should not have occurred
but did

I am made strong by the neglect
of what should have happened
but did not

Be prepared, fully prayed up and ready
because when purpose calls
Instinct will either have you run to it
or run from it

I have known since my adolescence
that the system is designed to fail

But I know
God, Universe and Nature shall see that I overcome

And when you die,
 you can take nothing with you

Sometimes, it does not matter
how hard you pray, hope or wish
the answer is no

And there is no explanation
and you have to accept
the situation for what it is

I can sense that a great blessing
is near but right now
I walk through dry bones

I must conquer in the valley
before I can reign on the mountain top

To be victorious
I must move past all that I see
faith, don't fail me now

Happy Life

He is a hardworking man
but today he punched out early
in a hurry to see his stunning wife

With the next four days off
he plans to make up for all the days he missed
and leaving her alone for many nights

A stop at the florist then the liquor store
romance is on his mind

Called from the office to order dinner
and everything is going fine

Turns on the radio, finds a song he likes
singing off-key, he butchers the verse

He loosens his tie and accelerates
so happy to be out of work

A few minutes later he picks up the food
and places it on the passenger seat

He's ready to please be it making love
or tenderly rubbing her feet

His promotion paid for the house
her sweet touch decorated their home

Waiting for her to respond to a text he sent
he takes a quick glance to see
there are no alerts on his phone

He arrives home places the food on the counter
cradles the flowers and holds on to the wine

He opens the bottle, pours two glasses
then he calls her name but hears no reply

After venturing upstairs he stops abruptly
devastated and shocked to hear a man grunt
accompanied by familiar sighs and moans

He walks to their bedroom door unable to believe
she violated their bed and marriage
by welcoming another man into their home

He drops the flowers, descends to the kitchen
and quickly returns with a large cut-co knife

Heartbroken a tear rolls down his cheek
his world is shattered
he was betrayed and now his mind ain't right

He kicks open the door
enraged by the scene in front of him
everything fades to red

A young man having his way with his wife
blowing her back out, defiling their sacred bed

He strikes quick with malice
through screams from the lovers
as he cuts with fury again and again

Once his rage subsides he kneels down to cry
after taking the secret lovers lives to a brutal end

He has no hope, he just murdered two people
he's going to prison
and he knows he ain't built for that hell

He kisses the blood on her forehead and tells her goodbye
then plunges the bloody knife deep into his chest

Mimi's Match

Forgive me if I am wrong
this feels like right

When your trapped in darkness
      you long for light

So much pain has become normal
I'm ready for something new

I'd given up on love
I was chasing success
then along came you

If this situation was different
do you think you and I would work?

I was left for dead, you make me feel alive
when it comes to love I feel like I'm cursed

Our commonalities are crazy our chemistry is intense
it's written all over your face

Time will tell if this is more than a feeling
until then all I can do is wait

This connection is natural the attraction grows deeper
I feel it when I look in your eyes

You have a boyfriend and I respect boundaries
but you've impacted my life

I am a fool for falling for you
knowing you are with someone else

We grew close but never crossed the line
now I want you for myself

We made magic you are in my heart
and I don't want to let you go

We talked about life we shared our dreams
you touched me deep in my soul

Eagles fly with eagles
love is tested I came back from a long way gone

When I'm with you I am happy
you make me feel like I'm not alone

You're deeper than the ocean you have gifted hands
I love your smile and you make me laugh

I wonder do you love him because I need you
I've finally met my match

So Be It

I trace every scar
they are chapters
in the story of my life

I'm grinding hard but it's all vanity
My goal is to leave an inheritance
to my offspring and descendants when I die

I am grateful and yes I am blessed
many don't get a second chance

I hear your spirit calling you know my heart
but I am just a man

I pray that your grace and protection
continue to reign over me

Anoint my hands, touch all that I do
give me the words to speak

I shall not let fear hinder me
for I am covered under your blood

Be my refuge draw me closer to you
when the adversary invades like a flood

I am not a hypocrite I'll admit when I am wrong
but my desire is to do right

Darkness calls as darkness falls
so I need you to shed your light

Bless my comrades
my team and everyone that I love
allow me to help somebody else

I pray for those that are waiting to see me fail
I wish every-one of them well

I can feel change coming
I'm so far from where I was
please don't give up on me

I have a long ways to go
but I'm on the right path
Keep me nearer my God to thee

Let Us Pray

God Bless America
and every place else!

This world is in peril
Lord, we need your help!

Anger, impatience, and unrest are growing stronger
evil is all around

White supremacists and Antifa will continue to clash
even though forty-five was voted out

Cowards slide until judgment
heroes are laid to rest

We're all contradictions
not everyone can accept change
and many of us live with regret

All I have is my word
so I speak from my heart

It will be wonderful when we can finally embrace
but for now, COVID 19 keeps us apart

Is this the book of Revelations being revealed
is the Beast rising before us?

Compassion is dying a slow death
much of humanity is being tortured

Blue lives matter? All lives matter?

As black man I'm beyond fed up with institutionalized racism
countless injustices and the execution of my people
most of whom were unarmed
So I declare with conviction, Black Lives Matter!

Oppressors and colonizers understand loss of resources
loss of capital and war, few revolutions have been successful
     without violence

SARS brutality, children are trafficked in the sex trade,
gentrification and the unloved suffer in silence

We search for something more
something of substance, something greater

Even if your heart is good with pure intentions
you will still encounter haters

Even when it looks hopeless
we must exhaust all possibilities to find a way

The sunken place is real
people perish there every day

There are too many invisible barriers
let us break the chains and demolish constructed walls

Deep division poisons heart and minds, and retards the moral
     compass
leading dynasties to an inevitable fall

We face segregated education along with
targeted areas plagued with high rates of unemployment and
     extreme poverty
as we endure a justice system that is broken and a painful joke

Death to all the lying prophets
that defile temples
telling lies and selling hope

God Bless America
and everyplace else!

This world is in peril
God we need your help!

No Chance

My resolve is absolute, my faith is unwavering

as I look past all that I see

I remain humble because I finally got back up

And I challenge the mighty to protect the weak

Obedience is better than to sacrifice

believes the man that gave his heart

You laid with the jackal, blood is on your hands

now regret tears you apart

Warnings are all around us

But we often allow arrogance, ego, and greed

to blind us to what's right in front of our face

Words can be misleading, eloquent words can deceive

but actions can lead to consequences that can't be erased

My love is eternal but my love is unable to reach you in hell

where torment reigns and fire burns

      Perhaps our paths will cross again

But for now, I live until Deaths Angel tells me it's my turn

Free Will

As a child, I knew Mattel, Nerf,
Hasbro, Nintendo, and Tonka

Kids today know apps,
Facetime, social media
and directed reality dramas

When I react with furious anger
it contradicts the good that I do
and the positive things that I say

I am human just like you
my outlook and emotion varies
the constant in life is change

Change isn't always easy
and at times unpleasant
I am told that change is good

I can't go back to fix the messes I've caused
many nights I'm robbed of sleep
wishing that I could

Still I make strides to be a better man
and make the most
out of the rest of my life

And when it is time for my soul
to pay for all of my sins
I will accept my plight

Love is irrelevant to a hardened heart
I hope my sons grow to be
better men than me

I choose not to complain
evolve, adapt or die
If I can be made whole
one day I can live free

Perspective Of Life

I am the sum total of a brave heart, a lost soul
a free spirit and a twisted mind
Faith is relevant only if you believe

And I believe so I must do
passion absent of purpose or focus
is an unwritten recipe for self-destruction

I will not entertain jubilee
while the kingdom suffers violence
and if the violent take it by force,
how dare I entertain pacifism?

Failure, rejection and crazy choices
fertilize my seed to destiny

I'm seeing firsthand that
the road less traveled is not an open road
however, here I can center myself in my lane
a shelter from the overcrowded rat-race

I make my way to higher ground
and find refuge from the flood
from this vantage point
I have a perfect shot of the devil I know

But I will not become lax in my elevation
for life has taught me
that new levels bring new devils

For everything there is a season
today I will enjoy this bountiful harvest
and have a hearty feast before the famine

And when the devastating storm comes
I will be ready
so I laugh hard now
because my teardrops are not far away

Flowers For Sandy
(An Amazing Woman that gives her all for so many)

Thank you for not aborting me
and keeping me after giving me life

I understand now, how you sacrificed
in doing your best to raise me right

Thank you for teaching me about Jesus
and showing me how to pray

Thank you for loving me unconditionally
when I hit rock bottom and lost my way

I can't thank you enough nor can I repay
All you've given to me and all that you do

It is a wonderful blessing
having you for a mother
from the depths of my heart

Sandy, I love you

Magic Killer

Dearest Love it is with a heavy heart
that I must detach myself from you
We've tried to dance time and time again
now the vinyl has been cracked cracked
      finally our songs gone off
You make me weak blinding me with a false hope
I don't have enough room for you
because you consume all of me
leaving no space or time
for my passion, calling or goals
I put you first always
and I am left wanting much more
I will not miss you
I have no regret, I turn my back
      after a swift sever, we are now detached
      I am free from the strings that tug on my heart
      Get from here!
and move on to anybody else

Sometimes
(D.F.L.)

True friends are hard to come by
and I only have a few

If you rode with me in the Caprice
or took turns driving the Dakota, then I'm talking about you

Sometimes the cost for greatness is not monetary or tangible
and you don't necessarily have to sell your soul

But you either confront or reconcile with your inner demons
and your only options are to work hard and walk alone

Only God can deliver from evil
but grit keeps me proving that impossible is just a word
when my paths terrain is wicked and rough

It takes power to look forward to tomorrow
          when it appears that a firestorm of failure
leaves no choice but to give your dreams up

I stay distant and silent I hate to disappoint myself
          admitting to you that I messed up yet again

Sometimes I feel like I'm insane
for this process is merciless and arduous
but I know I'll achieve good success when this process ends

I don't dwell on yesterday
but sometimes I go back to when I was happy
but in my youth, there was too much that I could not see

I was content to work for someone else and get high and drunk,
chasing girls and raising hell
but the universe had a greater purpose for me

Yes I miss my dogs, I hold on to the good times
the curse balances the gift
it took so long but I've broken the spell

I have to build this platform to help many
and open up seats at the table
and when we get there, oh do I have a story to tell

Coma Red

Heavy rain beats down on me
as I stand in the dark alone

I feel like I'm trapped in purgatory
but a free spirit is meant to roam

The night sky holds a plethora of clouds
cut deep by the shining moon

I work hard, I pray for change
I hope things get better
but I can't shake this feeling of doom

What if tonight Heaven is crying for us
perhaps it can feel the world's pain

Maybe the view from up there is vile and offensive
what we've done to earth
is an abominate and a shame

There's no peace for the driven,
the wicked are shocked by Karmas coming
and the virtuous go from faith to faith and glory to glory

We all have secrets we will all have hard times in life
but tough times and resistance make a great story

Deception and betrayal, sisters that are close to me
Or are these tricks in my twisted mind

Love is patience, Love is loyalty, Love is true
all will be revealed with time
I am a fiend but I also have faith
I strive to be righteous while I own heathen traits
I need to get right
I need to change enough
to walk through those pearled gates

I won't shave my beard
my temple is polluted
still I long to soar

After I climb to the top of a tall shaky ladder
that barely holds my weight
I arrive at another locked door

I think for a minute
then put a plan together
it all comes to me rather quick

I back up a few feet and get a running start
and I knock the door down with a mighty kick

Once through the door I'm outside and
heavy rain beats down on me
yet again, I stand alone

God damn,
I'm trapped in purgatory
with this free spirit
that is dying to roam

Definition

I am passion, I am pain, I am anger
I am driven, I am rejection, I am compassion,
I am rage, I am afraid, I am insecure, I am brave

In revealing that I must also confess,

I have tried, I have failed, I have triumphed, I have quoted
    scriptures, I have violated
I have been punished, I have been tormented, I have been a coward
    I have been heroic, I have been incarcerated, I have been freed

And having lived through all of that,

 I will not dwell on my past
because my destiny lies in my hands
I will appreciate each day I live to see
I will be the light as I walk this dark path

For I am committed, I am determined,
I am tattooed with many scars
However I still have hope, faith
and blessed with grit
and even if I fail, I will keep learning

And fully embrace everything that
I am

Fade

Exhausted, perplexed, and afraid
I think of Hamlet, Macbeth, and Othello
Three tragedies, three men that met a brutal end
by the workings of either their own demons
or the evil in those close to them
My thoughts, hopes, and ambitions
are teetering on the edge of madness
or is it hope?
I must survive this dreadful season
or is it my fate to perish
as wasted talent and all my effort and work die in vain?
 I guess only God knows
It is past midnight and as dense fog hovers
so does my apprehension of what is to come
I have no choice but to stay this course
and play out this real-life drama
I pray that I overcome this awful chapter in my life
and avoid my demise in a vicious travesty
However, I cannot ignore the fact
that history is prone to repeat itself
I guess I won't know until this scene ends

What Now?

So many lies so many whys so many tries
so much torment when there's nowhere to hide

Tomorrow will be much like today and yesterday
innocents will be slain, children will be abused
and wives will get beat

Fools will fall in love, survivors will overcome
and parents will hustle to make ends meet
In attempts to get ahead, I often come up short
but I'm good because I know all it takes is one

What matters most is how you finish
when it's all said and done

Political correctness is strictly enforced
the blanket of sexual misconduct has been pulled back
and turmoil resides in the White House

What's done in the dark will come to light
Our sins will find us out?

So many tries so many lies so many whys
so much torment when there's nowhere to hide

Unrest, envy, anger, and hatred seek to infect all within reach

In this country armed white terrorist are arrested peacefully
while unarmed black men are shot dead in the streets

Protests and riots, scandals and backlash, the rich get richer
and the poor continue to suffer

What happened to the times when the whole village raised a
child and we not only prayed for but looked out for one another?

Now is the time to stand to fight it only gets worse
damnation is coming souls will be taken

Do you believe in God?
Where will you run when the oceans rise high
and irreparable destruction is awakened?

So many whys so many tries so many lies
so much torment when there's nowhere to hide

Part 2

I cuss and you scream
we make up and repeat
I can't stay I can't leave
we fell way too deep
I love you

Whether wrong or right
you are my life
I want you by my side
a part of me
still feels like I need you

Life goes on
and we change
yet I still feel the same
I just want you to know
I miss you

So Gone

I levitate in the eye of the storm of desire, passion and love
arms wide open is a sweet comfort to a lonely heart
The mind attacks what does not appear logical to the parameters
of its depth
the heart will never cease to want what the heart wants
And the spirit will engage in continuous battle with the lusts of
the flesh
the magnificent voice of an earth angel led me to reminisce
And on that sleepless night, I longed for tender intimate
interaction
I chose to detach myself from the lost ones that fed their dark
matter with my energy
I care for you truly but I must turn my back to you forever
as the vultures feast on rotten carcasses, I appreciate being very
much alive
Inspiration comes in various forms; a hero must first face the
monster within
for there is a season for all things even the distasteful, frustration
and misery
Have I gone mad for ignoring the ominous signs and holding on
to hope as I refuse to turn back?
my faith paints me as a fool and my strength is to blame for my
agony
My comrades have either been slaughtered or scattered
utterly alone I embark on a quest to find peace of mind

And if I fail at least I'll learn how to survive through the valley of sorrow

Off Key

Sometimes the joy lies inside the pain

and you search for an answer that can't be explained

Just because I think or feel it, doesn't mean that I have to say it

when you only get one shot, you better make it

Water can't extinguish a fire that burns within one's soul

I'm okay with the voices inside my head, as long as they don't

take control

I'm not afraid of getting dirty and I am capable of handling myself

I don't mind isolation, I've grown accustomed to rejection

but I refuse to be silenced or shelved

The nature of survival will devour the weak, evolution is absolute

honor among thieves is deceptive, would you rather be a coward

or a fool?

Even though this situation is ugly the word says it's working out

for my good

I have been in love, wrong, and hated

oh how I hate being misunderstood

Outsider, rebel, and misfit are all parts of me

it takes great fortitude to be diligent when darkness is all you see

Thick skin is a necessity to endure, be wise and dress for the

weather

am I crazy for attempting to fly, being born without any feathers?

True friends are few, comrades depart and some battles last forever

Life is crazy, some things never change

and sometimes you do things that you swore you'd never

StarScream

We never walk alone
even when we can't see God

and it seems like he does not
 hear our prayers, he is there

Sometimes God's will is for our affliction
and he allows torment to come
in various situations and conditions

I give thanks in good times
I offer up praise in bad
I make the most of another day
for I am not here by chance

You gave me strength
I am full of love
as I continue on with courage

Better must come
because we're witnessing some of the worst
so much of what I see is disturbing

I wrestle with fear, worry and doubt
I'm still standing
but man I am tired

Sometimes purification will only occur
through baptism by fire

I must give
and I give all of me
for it is written
that much is required

The struggle is constant
as the spirit clashes with

my carnal desires

The good that I should do
often escapes me
I stand before you a perfect mess

I am hard on myself
I should have tried harder
we all live with regret

I know my breakthrough is on the way
it's just moving at a snail's pace

Forgive my sins, failures
short- comings, pride and every mistake

When passion aligns with purpose
destiny's road will be revealed

Never give up or give in
regardless of how bad
you may feel

I accept blessings and battles
I will fight until victory or defeat
I live through war and peace

Predators often lurk in high grass
most of life's lessons are not cheap

Unify us Oh Lord as we drop our egos
and obsessions with trying to get bigger

We're on the same team
we must work together
after all we are brothers and sisters

Renew my spirit, heal my troubled mind
let your presence hover from above

My hope is built

from all that I have left
courage, strength and love

Reflection

I'm damned if I do
but I'll die if I don't
I am such a magnet to
the things that hurt me the most
I sense she's far away
as we lay so close
I keep scriptures in my head
I talk to God when I smoke
There's no rest for the wicked
there's no light in this cave
My thoughts attack my spirit
for my thoughts are depraved
What I know of love
got me stabbed in the heart
Holding everything together
was ripping me apart
To live is to suffer
peace is hard to maintain
Coalitions of Panthera-leo fear nothing
except fire or a cage
Hatred spreads like poverty grass
and division grows
Doubt has overwhelmed me
it has me by my throat
I can feel the heat rising
I am ready to explode
I'm damned if I do
but I'm dead if I don't

Madness

I've been told that perception is reality
if that is true then reality is sublime
If you take a look around and see
what is really going on in this world,
it is apparent that we,
the inhabitants of this planet have gone utterly mad

There is an overabundance of violence,
death, destruction, inconsideration and disrespect
jealousy and envy are at an all-time high

Lack of self-love and hopelessness
seem to reign uncontested and unstoppable

If I had wings I would fly above the stratosphere
and hover over this carnage that we have created
endorsed and accepted

Unfortunately,
me being a romantic does not change what is real
and what is true

Time is moving too fast
and I cannot control my emotion
or the evil that is transpiring all around me

So I run to the mirror and I pause for just a moment
I look in the mirror and I am surprised to see a face
that I have not seen in a very long time

When I lock eyes with this man in the mirror
I am apprehensive and before I can turn away he smiles at me

This moment is awkward because I haven't seen this face in years

and the last time I did, we had a terrible fall out
Honestly, I didn't know if I'd see his face again

Somehow I find the courage to face this man
and I strike up a conversation

before long we are laughing
and we enjoy camaraderie with each-other like we did so long ago

Matter of fact,
we get so deep into conversation and catching up
  it's almost like the fall out never happened

Suddenly he looks at me with a serious face and says
"I always knew you would come back"
At this point I am puzzled and I reply "You were the one that left"

"No" he says "You pushed me away, I never left you,
I just fell back, man I was always here,
it made me sick watching the way you were living,
you were destroying yourself just like society is destroying
      this world "

After hearing that I am humbled and I feel blessed

I look back at him not knowing what to say
He interrupts my silence and says
"Man you don't have to say anything
it's really good to see you smiling again"

We talk for a little while longer
until I notice the time and remember
that I have to get ready for work

I ask him, when will I see you again?
He chuckles and answers
"My brother, that's completely up to you"
I tell him, "Fair enough"

Before I say goodbye, he says to me

"Hey, I want you to look at this world and your life,
if a man can change for the better,
he can make his world a better place"

I leave the mirror
to prepare myself for the long work day ahead
and it sinks in that as human beings,
we can only control our own actions

However, if we loved ourselves to the fullest
and had respect for our own quality of life and well-being
we would contemplate the results of our actions
before we reacted with anger hatred or disrespect

And we would not have time for jealousy or envy
because we would all be making moves to make this world a
    better place
Death and destruction are a part of life
sometimes the good die young and destruction befalls good people
 those facts are sad and hard to accept or explain

 Respect is earned but if we had more respect for our-selves,
 then we would have more respect for each-other and life
then maybe there would not be as much violence
and maybe death would not be so senseless

Maybe not,
maybe I am as mad as the rest of this world
I do believe that hope is not lost

Now I am not arrogant or naïve enough to think
that I can save/change this world or anybody else
all I can do is save my world
and hope that others have the desire to save theirs

So please
cohabitants of this world respect yourselves and love yourselves
live your lives and leave no room in your heart for hate

envy or jealousy toward one another.

And consider the fact that too many of our young
are meeting their demise by senseless violence
only together can we halt this mad worlds destruction

J.D.

We laughed and learned together
you were my best friend
With rings we vowed forever
I thought we'd never end
Tonight I lay alone
and you are miles away
Who would have thought forever
would turn out this way?

Far Out

Fly away fly away
don't look back

Fly above all the hatred
all the violent attacks

To a place of understanding
to a land of peace

Where time's insignificant
and it's uncommon
to feel grief

A realm beyond this insanity
world that the wicked can't control

A place where I belong
and I can finally call home

Mid Life

To me rejection is motivation
so I am okay with being overlooked
pushed away and refused

For in due time prominence will bestow
Understanding and believing this
I pray for continued patience and humility

I am grateful for the understanding to know

That it is better to help elevate
by being a stepping stone
than to cause a downfall
by being a stumbling block

Is There Not A Cause?

The power of life and death lies in the tongue
for many it's harder to get a job
than it is to get a gun

If you're standing on the edge
think hard before you jump
They call us toxic males
to make future generations of punks

We will never have unity until we stand as one
woe to the man that blatantly kills for fun
Are we in the last days?
Has the Great Tribulation begun?
Is there not a cause?

A new world order is being constructed
with an agenda of evil, perversion, and destruction
Change is trapped in red tape, lies, and corruption
now is the time to assemble
instead of standing reluctant

Do you remember when that dentist killed Cecil the lion
and much of the world wanted to hang that man
Yet to this day there are no convictions
in the murder of Sandra Bland

Cells of upheaval germinate all over this land
we must come together, Lord help us understand
Without you we're lost and we don't stand a chance
God deliver us from evil, out of Satan's grasp
Is there not a cause?

Where are all my friends
where did my comrades go?
I was forsaken by the one
that vowed she'd love me the most

Some seeds become trees
so watch the seeds that you sow
If they slaughter our babies
then the future can't grow

Search for the answers
for all the things that you don't know
Don't let the controlled media persuade you
to give up faith and hope
Is there not a cause?

You must be a student
before you can teach
Champions are made
after they suffer defeat

If the bar is set high
then the fall is steep
Predators come to annihilate
and devour the weak

Greed and jealousy make things seem like
there will never be peace
War is everywhere, hatred runs deep
Is there not a cause?

A racial divide is set to tear us apart
Intolerance, ignorance, and fear
whip this country hard

How are we moving backward
when we've come so far?
Brothers and sisters we are leaders
when will we take charge?

Work, watch, fight, and pray
we must stay on guard
Let us uphold the light
so it shines through the dark
        I ask you,
Is there not a cause?

No Room For Error

As I think so am I
Inspiration didn't smite me
until I was rejected

God wakes me up
Pride keeps me going
and I wonder
if I am either detached or disconnected

My cold lonesome nights
were extensions of long hard days

I never would have made it this far
if I didn't learn how to pray

The system was designed for failure
by bad intentions and evil schematics

To evolve I must transform my mind
change my energy
and put an end to toxic habits

I am chasing success
I work hard to live my dream
with a will, I shall not let die

These words from my soul
validate the passion that burns within
A Blessing and purpose
given by the Most High

I will do my best
I embrace tests
I've learned not every loss is a failure

I am not easily broken
there's ice in my veins

and I have never felt better

Redemption has renewed my strength
I can almost break these chains

The joy I feel is a fortress
from pain that comes at me in waves

I expect the best to come from my worst
being at my worst was motivation
for me to do and be my best

No one sees me coming
and that's great for I am gaining ground
I am way too hungry to rest

I climbed from the bottom
now I stand at the precipice
laughing in the face of terror

I am claiming everything
or nothing at all
which leaves me
No room for error

Cycle Of Carnage

A well-placed move
followed by a letting down
of one's guard could lead to
Reaping and remorse

A reaping quite grim
that leaves wounds on souls
malevolent and merciless

Birthing bastard spawns
Of poor, miscalculated,
selfish, foolish, decisions

Spawns mighty enough to demolish
even a strong man's mental
Spawns with the power to burrow
deep into a man's core
laying dormant for years

Only to manifest in future generations
wrecking mayhem on the bloodline
for generations to come

My Girl

The radiant glow
on her face allure me
and the spark in her pretty
green eyes intrigue me

Her silly cackle of a laugh
never fails to force a grin on my face

She enjoys wrapping her arms around my neck
breast on chest, abdomen against stomach
as we hug too long and way too close

It is my pleasure to move in closer
as our body heat turns up
and for a spell, we become trapped in slow motion

The attraction is intense
she is a romantic
turned on by possibilities
I am drawn to her energy
touch and strength

When she talks I listen
our chemistry is great
and the vibe between us grows deeper

She's intelligent, caring, and driven
and possesses a great sense of humor
Open minded and full of life
she's oblivious to her incredible sex appeal

She takes good care of her body
as well as her mind
her profile and form outline a red dress well

She is into sports and she loves to cook
I'd be a fool not to make
this pretty young thing my own

 She gives her body to me
to fulfill the attention she lacks
from the man she loves at home

Harvest Time

I would pay
to see a tiger
that could erase his stripes

It's sad to say
but many fuckups
will never ever get right

To beat the odds
fight harder, get stronger
and move faster

If greatness is within you
adversity and opposition won't matter

True friends are few,
loyalty is rare
love will show

Family, vices and the past
can be hard to let go

If ever you're ready to give up
I want you to remember this

And that is
this world is cruel, sometimes you'll lose
but don't you ever quit

Here We Are Again

It was a hell of an election
I felt an odd sense of hope
witnessing the address after
Biden and Harris were voted in

Does social media hurt more than it heals?
When will this madness end?
Violence claims victims all over the world
when will peace begin?

The more we separate, the more we lose
if we unify we will win
Injustice, protests the fight goes on
here we are again

Do you hear the rhetoric
from the far left and the alt right?
When will we have
an effective prison reform?

It is your right to be whatever you want
but it is unconstitutional to silence freedom of speech
Do you agree with canceling or muting platforms?

Some want reparations
others want closed borders
I am sick and tired of seeing my people killed

The whole world is watching **US**
emotions and tensions are super high
it feels like a second civil war could break out for real

Yes, I want my country to be great
but must we refer to our past?

Is it acceptable to listen to entertainers and athletes
used to endorse candidates and capture votes
but allow a proven brother
with a solid plan to be attacked?
(I stand with Cube)

We've prayed
marched and rioted
a sense of entitlement receives no respect

Let's compare all of our wants
to what we really need
deal with facts and keep our feelings in check

We can agree to disagree
but to debate we must first
be clear on what the argument is about

Will we allow xenophobia
to dictate immigration laws?
Should we welcome undocumented immigrants
or should we throw them all out?

I truly believe that better
will come one day
the burning question is when

We fight among ourselves
trying to make sense of all that has gone wrong

Yes, here we are again

Stunner

Homicide, genocide, suicide
we live in such strange times
where good and evil coincide

No one is perfect
I am perfectly flawed

The fire of vengeance is spreading
Payback sometimes leaves us appalled

A lie is a comfort
To those that won't accept the truth

I will follow no one
I will protect my mind from contamination
        with a free will I will choose

It is good to honor your spiritual leader
but depend on no man
to interpret God in thee

You better stand and get bad
or get brutally violated
on your hands and knees

Pain

Coach: Bird he's destroying you out there

Bird: I got him right where I want him

Coach: I don't know how you got through that last round. How in the world are you still standing?

Bird: By the grace of God and the skin of my teeth

Coach: Bird, I'm ready to throw in the towel

Bird: Hell no!

Coach: He's stronger than you, faster than you, he's deadly and a better fighter.

Bird: I know Coach, you're very observant

Coach: There are only three rounds left and he's ahead in points. You'll have to win all three just for the decision to be close

Bird: Don't worry; we won't need a decision because I'm going to put him down this round

Coach: What the hell are you talking about? Look at you

Bird:(Laughing) Do I look that bad?

Coach: He's beating the brakes off of you

Coach: Bird, you're like a son to me I can't watch you get killed!

Bird: Coach, this is bigger than a fight, this is my life, I'll keep fighting no matter how this turns out

Coach: Boy, you're crazy just like your brother

Bird: Well, being that I'm older I'd say my brother is crazy like me and furthermore my brother wouldn't be losing this fight

Coach: True enough but this ain't about your brother, it's about you

Bird: Coach, this I know

Coach: If you want to go through with this I'm with you but you're risking not only your career but possibly your life

Bird: I told you I'm good

Bird: I need you to do two things

Coach: What?

Bird:(rises off stool) Put my mouthpiece in

Coach: Alright, what else?

Bird : Get ready to celebrate a huge upset and great comeback

Coach: God be with you, Bird

Ding Ding

Unbelievable

When we lock eyes you feel it
so show me something real
other than empty promises
smiling faces and hidden agendas

Blessings are coming
right after dog days, all types of trials
exhaustion and dilemmas

God's will be done
Principalities rule this earth
I'd rather know how
There are too many variables for
me to understand why

We all hate failing
not everyone deserves to win
Woe to the shiftless
that won't even try

We rarely accept what we don't understand
If heaven is truly above earth
Then evil came from on high

I'll shed a tear for anyone
born this day
and I'll laugh hard
for those that will die

Flash

Doing all that I know to succeed
each setback fuels my inner doubts
that quickly flows through my veins

In my lifetime the world has changed
there's a huge market for immorality
still my principles remain

A seasoned rebel
imaginative, creative
giving, twisted, a bit dark
and I wouldn't be mad if you called me strange

So many think they know love
and many more want to be loved
But love don't fix crazy
and it don't always cover pain

God give me the strength to keep going
give me the wisdom to know how to move
and grant me peace when you call my name

These words, everything I record and all I capture
will live on after I am dead and gone
spread my ashes then destroy the urn
a final victory over the grave

Break Away

One stolen kiss
a final goodbye

The crocodile tear
makes a slow descent
from your glistening eye

Do you believe in fate?
Have you sold your soul?

My conscious is clear
my blood runs cold

I try not to lie
I used to steal

I keep to myself
I hope I never have to kill

I hide then I chase
and I end up wanting

Solitude is routine
I've grown accustomed to longing

When Destiny calls
even if it puts me in danger
straight to it I will run

I am not nearly as fast as I used to be
yet somehow I will catch up

Forever And Ever And

I wanted to be like Jesus
until I got sick of them whooping my ass

I was far from cool
skipped many days of school
that's why it took so long to pass

The chip on my shoulder became so heavy
it was putting a strain on my back

Feelings change like the wind
Betas execute off emotion
Beliefs can't argue with facts

Alert, sober and alone
well past the midnight hour
plotting and strategizing like a clever devil

Poor planning will lead to the fall
then there will be no mercy at all
I will scavenge and survive the peril

Maybe my outlook is wrong
trust, I couldn't care less
I walk alone and I watch my own back

No one will want the smoke
when the inferno consumes
and all that was
is reduced to memories and ashes

Highway

Liberated spirits mate with lost souls
some will bask in indescribable joys
while others die slow from broken hearts

Balance is celebrating in
intoxicating winning seasons
and enduring miserable losing streaks

Some make their mark in history
through ruthless aggression
others change narratives
through nonviolence

There are many ways
to find Universal God
as are a plethora of highways to hell

It was with the best intentions
that I fucked everything up

In my lifetime
temporary relief deals best
with my pain

Through circumstance troubled men
are forced to evolve in dark times

Motivated I move fast and forward
while in my heart
there's a longing to rewind

273

Flesh and spirit fail to find common ground
causing us to fall
            further away from the objective
and ever hopelessly out of sync

The discord mirrors this ludicrous world
a planet-size stage
for this asinine reality

The Most High gave me a gift
to share with the world
In my youth my roots were planted in the church
from time to time I miss that atmosphere

And it's tough because I know that it's in me
but for a while now
I feel like it ain't me

And even though I am unworthy and unqualified
            these words, songs and stories
run marathons through my mind and soul

With hands covered in blood, dirt, and sweat
I built an altar, and through labor, time, and love
I offer a sacrifice of thanks and praise

This tiny garden
a dedication to the universal God
designed to feed and nourish his children

The tabernacle is built and fortified
on and in good soil
Observing the healthy produce grow well

I am grateful for these hallowed grounds
the aura from this small plot of vegetables
provides peace and contentment

A natural relief
and also motivation to keep going
when on many days and nights
I contemplate ending it all

In a perfect world, I could bottle this
and keep it with me
as an antidote for hard times

Unfortunately, this is far from a perfect world
however,
knowing that I have a place to run to
a place where life grows
an organic utopia of serenity

Is enough to breathe fresh air
onto the embers of smoldering faith
and prepare me

For whatever battle
accompanies this upcoming blessing
and bountiful harvest

God give me the words and vision
to create art that accurately depicts
such a beautiful piece of my life

Coming To

It seems like all I do is
        work hard, smoke and think
        No peace, I barely eat
        It's hard to sleep

I'm haunted by empty promises
        and to my grave unholy secrets
        I'll keep

God,
open my eyes
        touch my unbelief

Just because I've accepted
        what is
        does not mean
This is what it has to be

If I don't evolve
        and continue on the same path
        the road ahead looks bleak

Change is vital
adapt or perish
        Total restoration is in need

My past is in the past
        Destiny will fulfill tomorrow
        so I focus on right now

God I know you hear me
        you see my effort and heart
        Please make a way for me somehow

Above the darkness and the pain
      and the legion and the rage
and everything else that steals my peace

This dreaded low place is not my home
      I don't belong here
      There's so much better in me

Just a tiny mustard seed
has the power to produce
      roots, strong, solid and deep

I'm starting to feel better

I don't need to smoke
      my mind is at ease
      But now I am incredibly hungry
and I want something to eat

And after that
      I will lay down
and fall deep into a good night's sleep

Afterword

I am humbled and honored that you entered my world

I hope you enjoyed this collection and were able to take
something away from it

Life is crazy and so much is happening in this world.

Please open your eyes and mind to appreciate the beauty of the
small things in life.

I pray that you are able to understand the significance of the
storms through the process in your journey

Please make healthy and wise decisions and take good care of
yourselves

Make time to enjoy life, because when it's over it's over!

I appreciate your support! God Bless!

Appreciation and Respect

Thank you to: my brothers, friends, and comrades Timothy, David, Brandon, Darrell Strozier, Joseph Newborn, Demetrius Bennett, Jason Singletary, Terrance Winbush. Thank you for the encouragement, believing in me, and pushing me to keep fighting, writing, and going when I was at my lowest. The conversations, texts, time spent, prayers and support were priceless. Gentlemen, we did it! God Bless you all! Much respect, appreciation and love!

Oh, and I would be remiss if I didn't acknowledge Karma, my self-destructive tendencies, and everything designed or sent to slay me. Excellent effort...

Acknowledgments

Definition: First published in *Nine Cloud* journal

Hands Of War: First published in *Havik*

Just Thought I'd Share That With You: First published in *Maudlin House*

Long Shot: First published in *Havik*

Outsider: First published in *The Good Men Project*

Reflection: First published in *Finding the Birds*

Thank you to Submittable for creating a network that allows artist to create platforms.

Thank you to everyone at Atmosphere involved in this project!

About Atmosphere Press

Atmosphere Press is an independent, full-service publisher for excellent books in all genres and for all audiences. Learn more about what we do at atmospherepress.com.

We encourage you to check out some of Atmosphere's latest releases, which are available at Amazon.com and via order from your local bookstore:

Grafting, poetry by Amy Lundquist

How to Hypnotize a Lobster, poetry by Kristin Rose Jutras

Love is Blood, Love is Fabric, poetry by Mary De La Fuente

The Mercer Stands Burning, poetry by John Pietaro

Lovely Dregs, poetry by Richard Sipe

Meraki, poetry by Tobi-Hope Jieun Park

Calls for Help, by Greg T. Miraglia

Out of the Dark, poetry by William Guest

Lost in the Greenwood, poetry by Ellen Roberts Young

Blessed Arrangement, poetry by Larry Levy

Shadow Truths, poetry by V. Rendina

A Synonym for Home, poetry by Kimberly Jarchow

Big Man Small Europe, poetry by Tristan Niskanen

The Cry of Being Born, poetry by Carol Mariano

Lucid_Malware.zip, poetry by Dylan Sonderman

In the Cloakroom of Proper Musings, by Kristin Moriconi

It's Not About You, poetry by Daniel Casey

The Unordering of Days, poetry by Jessica Palmer

Radical Dances of the Ferocious Kind, poetry by Tina Tru

The Woods Hold Us, poetry by Makani Speier-Brito

About the Author

Nathaniel Terrell resides in Western NY. He is also a spoken word artist and creates content for his youtube channel and Reverb nation page. In 2014 he published an inaugural collection of poems titled *Here goes nothing* through Mylk "n" Honee Publishing. Other of his work has been in publications including *Cram Journal*, *Writing Raw*, *Fine Line Journal*, *Good Men Project*, *Maudlin House*, *Havik*, *Finding the Birds*, and *Nine Cloud Journal*.

Contact Nathaniel Terrell
watsedtalent79@yahoo.com
https://www.facebook.com/nathaniel.terrell.522
Instagram @life.mid (Nathaniel Terrell)